VEGETABLE GARDENING FOR BEGINNERS

A Beginner's Guide to Starting Your Own Vegetable Garden

Table of Contents

Chapter One
The Allure of Growing Your Own Food

Gardening is cheaper than therapy and you get tomatoes.
~Author Unknown

I can't think of a single person who would rather eat corn out of a can than fresh corn on the cob. I also don't know anyone who would rather eat a tomato that traveled hundreds of miles to get to the store than one picked by a local farmer the day before. Do you?

The question of why we prefer fresh is a no-brainer. Taste. Nutritional value. Overall quality. These are the obvious reasons, but the main reason is one we usually don't even mention. It's what I'll call 'satisfying our inner farmer.' There's just something right about growing our own food. It could just be a couple pots of fresh herbs on the windowsill in the kitchen, or a tomato plant growing outside the back door. Or it might be a full-fledged garden complete with tomatoes, peppers, lettuce, green beans, and maybe even some squash and corn. Big or small, there's a sense of satisfaction that comes from eating something we've grown with our own two hands (and a little help from nature).

The allure of gardening is undeniable, but there's a common misconception that you need a yard you can partially convert into a garden and two green-as-grass thumbs to get into it. It's true that, by and large, in-ground or raised bed gardens offer more options than container gardens, but...

- You *can* successfully garden in spaces smaller than you think.

- Container gardening will work as long as you stick to plants suitable for containers.

With very few exceptions, anyone can grow vegetables of their own. So, if raising some of your own food is on your bucket list, or something you want to do for the benefit of yourself and your family, you can be one of the 40% (give or take a percent or two) of American households that have a vegetable garden of some sort.

Gardening in the US

If you still aren't sure you have the space or skill to grow a few veggies for your table, take a few minutes to look at what the rest of America is doing. Of the 43 million Americans who grow some of their own food…

- 86% grow tomatoes

- 47% grow cucumbers

- 46% grow sweet peppers

- 39% grow green beans

- 32% grow summer squash

- 28% grow lettuce

- 24% grow sweet corn

Here are some other interesting gardening facts that will motivate you to start digging in the dirt:

- The average size of the family vegetable garden is 600 square feet (about 24x24 feet).

- The median size is 96 square feet (just under 10x10 feet).

- More women garden than men. Statistics show that 79% of people who raise their own vegetables are women.

- The average age of someone who gardens is 48. This shouldn't come as any surprise when you consider the following:

  – Generally speaking, people over the age of 35 have had more exposure to a rural and agricultural way of life.

  – Younger people tend to have less time to garden. They are too busy raising kids, taking kids to and from extra-curricular activities, and working to pay off student loans and reach their career goals.

- The area in which you live doesn't dictate whether or not you will be successful in your gardening venture. While some regions of the country are better for growing certain types of fruits and vegetables than others, the majority can be grown wherever you live. You just need to know that the growing seasons differ depending on the climate. (More on that later.)

The country is evenly divided in its love for gardening. If you were to divide the country into four different regions, you would find that between 22% and 29% of people in each region have a vegetable garden of some kind.

Chapter Two
Ready… Set…

Weather means more when you have a garden. There's nothing like listening to a shower and thinking how it is soaking in around your green beans. ~Marcelene Cox

Now that you've decided to try your hand at raising vegetables, you need to take some time to make sure you do it right. You know, make sure you have prepared your gardening space correctly, that you have the proper tools and equipment, and that you have a basic understanding of how to plant and care for the food you grow.

Preparing your garden space

No matter how big or small your garden is, and no matter what kind of garden you decide to have, preparing the space so that it is conducive for growing is a must. Preparing your garden space consists of the following:

- Decide how much room you have to devote to raising food.

- Decide what kind of garden will be most suitable for the space you have (in-ground, raised bed, or container).

- For in-ground gardens, you will need to peel the sod off the dirt, remove any rocks and remaining weeds, and break the soil using a hoe to a depth of about 6 inches.

- For in-ground gardens, you will need to add peat moss. You can buy bags or 'bales' of peat moss at any garden center or big box discount store with a garden department. You will need **one**

bale of peat moss per 100 square feet of garden space. To add the peat moss to your garden, scatter it around the surface and work it in using a spade and/or hoe.

- If you choose to build raised beds, the first thing you need to do after deciding how much area you'll be using, is decide what you will use to build the borders of your raised beds.

- Once the raised bed borders are in place, you need to fill the area with **garden soil and peat moss.** In similar fashion to an in-ground garden, you will need to work the soil and peat moss together using a spade and/or hoe.

- If you have chosen container gardening, the obvious first step is to select your containers. The main things to keep in mind are the size of the pot and its drainage capability.

- Preparing your pots for planting is easy. You simply fill them with **potting soil**—not garden soil, peat moss, or soil from your yard. Potting soil.

Aside from choosing the type of garden you'll have and its size, placement is also very important. Regardless of the type of garden you want, it will require ample sunshine, proper drainage, protection from critters, and access to water. Here are some tips on the placement of your garden:

- It will need 6 to 7 hours of sunlight each day (a southwest location in your yard is best).

- It should be on flat, level ground, and NOT located at the bottom of a hill where run-off will land.

- Avoid planting under trees that will give off too much shade and drop debris like falling leaves.

- You will want it to be near a water hydrant—close enough for a hose and sprinkler to easily reach the entire area.

- Your garden should be in an easy-access location, but also one that won't make mowing the rest of the yard difficult, infringe on the kids' play area, or be a problem for pets who like to romp in the yard.

- Consider putting a fence around the area to keep pets (yours or the neighbors') and other unwanted critters away.

Make sure you have the equipment you need

You know how some parents buy a Steinway when their six-year-old decides he or she wants to play the piano, or they spend $100 on soccer cleats or $50 on baseball pants for their 4-year-old's first tee-ball experience? Hopefully that's not you. Hopefully you kept your wits about you and realized that having only the finest equipment wasn't going to make them play any better. The same holds true with gardening. While there are some things you can't go without, you do NOT need the biggest, best, and most expensive of everything. Trust me, a $2 pair of gardening gloves can pull weeds just as well as a $20 pair, and a free or nearly free 5-gallon bucket with holes drilled into the bottom can be home to a tomato plant just as adequately as a $30 pot that matches your patio furniture.

Below is a list of the essential items you'll need to grow your own vegetables. The ones with an asterisk are items you need to purchase in terms of quality over cheapest available price. Those without asterisks are the items you can get from the dollar store or yard sales.

- Shovels (spade/sharpshooter and garden shovel)

- Hoe

- Rake

- Heavy-duty hose

Sprinkler- The simpler, the better, but it needs to be heavy enough to not jump or flip over when you turn the water on. Quality is important, but experience tells me you find the best sprinklers at estate auctions and moving sales and that you don't have to spend much to get a good one.

Plant stakes and markers- Craft sticks you write on with sharpies will do.

Watering can- As long as it has holes so you can 'rain' on your plants instead of just dumping water on them, anything will do.

- Potting soil- I'm not one to promote one brand over another, but there really is none better than Miracle Grow®.

- Garden soil (same as above)

- Garden gloves

- Garden shears (scissors)

- Tomato cages

Pesticide- It doesn't get any better than Dawn dish soap and water.

Fertilizer- I'll talk more about this later, but it's not necessary to spend a lot on fertilizer. Chances are you use plenty of stuff in your everyday life that you can use to fertilize your garden.

- Seed and seedlings- Quality seed is affordable.

Decide what to grow

Deciding what to grow in your garden is a matter of personal taste... literally. 😊 Just because the majority of people who raise vegetables raise tomatoes, doesn't mean you have to. If you don't like them, don't plant them. Besides that, there are two other things you need to take into consideration:

1. The size of your garden

   You can successfully grow *most* vegetables regardless of how big your in-ground or raised bed garden is, but not all. Things like corn, melons, pumpkins, and cucumbers (unless you train them to grow on a trellis) need lots of room.

   Container gardens are a bit more restrictive. Botanists have developed varieties of a large number of vegetables suitable for growing in containers. There are some, however, that simply won't work. Corn, pumpkins, okra, and asparagus are all examples of vegetables that don't fit into the container gardening picture.

   You also need to remember that not all varieties are alike. If you decide you want to grow some green beans in your container garden, you need to make sure you purchase seeds developed for container gardening. You also need to make sure you follow the guidelines for the size of container necessary. NOTE: guidelines are more than friendly suggestions.

2. The planting zone you live in

The following map shows planting zones. For the most part, the accuracy of the planting zone map is spot on. There will be exceptions at times, such as dates for first and last frost. Sometimes certain regions will have an early or late fall. For example, a couple of years ago, people in the Ozarks (a section of the Midwest) enjoyed a longer and milder growing season than usual. Many people who planted green beans in May to harvest in July replanted them in August and harvested them in October. What can I say? Nature does what it does, but these maps can certainly give you something to go by.

PLANTING ZONE

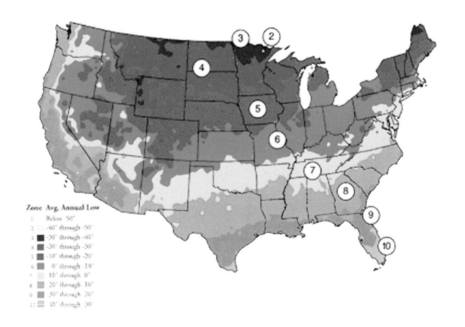

FIRST AND LAST FROST DATES

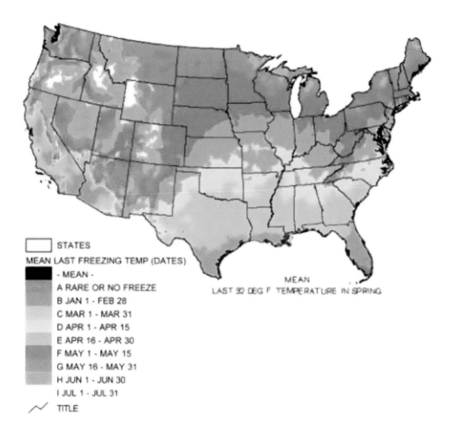

STATES

MEAN LAST FREEZING TEMP (DATES)

- MEAN -
A RARE OR NO FREEZE
B JAN 1 - FEB 28
C MAR 1 - MAR 31
D APR 1 - APR 15
E APR 16 - APR 30
F MAY 1 - MAY 15
G MAY 16 - MAY 31
H JUN 1 - JUN 30
I JUL 1 - JUL 31
TITLE

MEAN
LAST 32 DEG F TEMPERATURE IN SPRING

Chapter Three
Working the Ground So That it will Work for You

One of the most delightful things about a garden is the anticipation it provides. ~W.E. Johns

In the previous chapter we took an abbreviated look at what it takes to prepare the three main types of gardens for planting. In the next few chapters we're going to look at each one individually and talk about their specific pros and cons and offer a few suggestions on making your garden a joy and a success. After that, we'll look at a couple less traditional gardening techniques, and then we'll delve into the basics of planting and garden maintenance.

Are you ready? Let's get started.

In-ground gardening

I won't repeat everything I said earlier, but I want to remind you that your in-ground garden needs to be properly prepared (see previous chapter). Taking the time to do it correctly will make planting, maintaining, and harvesting your garden easier and more enjoyable. You will also harvest more from a well-kept garden than you will from one that isn't.

Assuming that your in-ground garden is in a good spot and has been properly prepared, now it is time to get down to business. Planting at the right time is essential. But what is the right time?

The right time to plant is after the last frost date for your zone, combined with the actual weather pattern. For example, if your zone's last frost date is between April 1 and 15, yet you are still experiencing nighttime temperatures that are near or below freezing, you need to hold off.

The right time to plant is when the soil is warm enough to nurture the plants instead of stunting them. A good rule of thumb is that your nighttime temperature needs to be 50 to 55 degrees F for a few days before planting seeds or seedlings outside (no matter what type of garden you have).

The right time to plant depends on the moon. Go ahead and laugh, but I know what I'm talking about—just like farmers and gardeners have known for centuries. Planting according to the moon's phase isn't a bunch of hocus-pocus or superstition. It is based on scientific evidence and was discovered long before science even existed.

Ancient peoples knew that the moon's phases affected the growth of plants, how livestock (and babies) did when it came to weaning them off their mothers, and a number of other things. How did they know? They learned from experience and intuition. They weren't ignorant. They paid attention to what was going on around them and used their observations for their own good.

Planting by the moon is not a complicated matter. Knowing which phase the moon is in is as easy as looking it up online and being able to count to thirty.

Vegetables that grow above the ground (corn, tomatoes, watermelon, peppers, peas, melons and zucchini, for example) should be planted during the **waxing** of the moon—from the day the moon is new to the day it is full. As the moonlight increases night by night, plants are encouraged to grow leaves and stems.

Plant **flowering bulbs, biennial and perennial flowers**, and **vegetables that bear crops below ground** (such as onions, carrots, and potatoes) during the **waning** of the Moon—from the day after it is full to the day before it is new again. As the moonlight decreases night by night, plants are encouraged to grow roots, tubers, and bulbs.

Once you decide what to plant you will need to plan your garden's layout. I know it may not seem like a big deal, but it is. There is a science of sorts for planting certain things together. It is called **companion planting.** Take a few minutes to look at the companion planting guides and follow them as closely as possible, based on the vegetables and herbs you want to plant.

FRIEND	FOE	FRIEND	FOE	FRIEND	FOE
BEANS		**CORN**		**ONIONS**	
Beets	Garlic	Beans	Tomatoes	Beets	Beans
Broccoli	Onions	Cucumbers		Broccoli	Peas
Cabbage	Peppers	Lettuce		Cabbage	Sage
Carrots	Sunflowers	Melons		Carrots	
Cauliflower		Peas		Lettuce	
Celery		Potatoes		Peppers	
Corn		Squash		Potatoes	
Cucumbers		Sunflowers		Spinach	
Eggplant				Tomatoes	
Peas		**CUCUMBERS**		**PEPPERS**	
Potatoes					
Radishes		Beans	Aromatic	Basil	Beans
Squash		Cabbage	herbs	Coriander	Kohlrabi
Strawberries		Cauliflower	Melons	Onions	
Summer		Corn	Potatoes	Spinach	
savory		Lettuce		Tomatoes	
Tomatoes		Peas			
		Radishes			
		Sunflowers			
CABBAGE		**LETTUCE**		**RADISHES**	
Beans	Broccoli	Asparagus	Broccoli	Basil	Beans
Celery	Cauliflower	Beets		Coriander	Kohlrabi
Cucumbers	Strawberries	Brussels		Onions	
Dill	Tomatoes	sprouts		Spinach	
Kale		Cabbage		Tomatoes	
Lettuce		Carrots			
Onions		Corn			
Potatoes		Cucumbers			
Sage		Eggplant			
Spinach		Onions			
Thyme		Peas			
		Potatoes			
CARROTS		Radishes		**TOMATOES**	
		Spinach			
Beans	Anise	Strawberries		Asparagus	Broccoli
Lettuce	Dill	Sunflowers		Basil	Brussels
Onions	Parsley	Tomatoes		Beans	sprouts
Peas				Borage	Cabbage
Radishes				Carrots	Cauliflower
Rosemary				Celery	Corn
Sage				Dill	Kale
Tomatoes				Lettuce	Potatoes
				Melons	
				Onions	
				Parsley	
				Peppers	
				Radishes	
				Spinach	
				Thyme	

Companion planting serves several purposes, some of which are obvious if you think about it. Others aren't so obvious but are equally beneficial. As you read through the reasons for companion planting, I hope you realize it is something you need to take seriously.

- Planting the right herbs with your veggies acts as a deterrent for many garden pests (bugs). The scent of the herbs scares many of the bad bugs away.

- Some taller plants provide just the right amount of shade for shorter plants.

- Plants like melons and cucumbers that crawl along the ground act as a weed-prevention mechanism for things like corn and okra, making overall management easier.

- Root crops pull nutrients up from a deeper part of the soil than ground crops. So, by planting potatoes and beets close to beans, zucchini, or several others from the list, your plants can actually feed each other.

- Plants don't all eat the same nutrients from the soil. As different plants pull different nutrients from the soil, it changes the balance in a good way. This is another way plants can help feed each other.

- A row of sunflowers can serve as a support for climbers like peas, mini gourds, and cucumbers.

Seeds or bedding plants? That is a question a lot of novice gardeners have. Will seedlings grow faster? Are seedlings easier than seeds?

Some vegetables can be started indoors and transplanted into the ground just fine. In fact, in many cases, transplanting young plants (usually referred to as bedding plants) is the best way to go. Using bedding plants, which are plants with 2 to 4 sets of leaves, greatly reduces the chances of 'baby' seedlings being eaten or trampled by wildlife and/or not tolerating a cold snap or excessive rain—both of which are common occurrences in the spring in many parts of the country.

Planting bedding plants doesn't have to take away from the experience of 'starting from scratch,' i.e. growing everything from seed. You will need to start your plants indoors 4 to 6 weeks prior to the time you want to plant your garden. To start your plants indoors, you will need a warm, sunny location you can dedicate to the cause. It needs to be a place you don't mind getting a little damp, as you will need to keep the soil warm and moist. As the seedlings pop through the soil you will find that occasionally misting the young plants will give them an added boost.

If you don't have the space or desire to start your plants from seed, don't worry. You will have plenty of options for buying bedding plants as soon as the growing season begins. No, I take that back. You'll have plenty of options for buying bedding plants even *before* the planting season should begin. I haven't decided whether it's a marketing ploy or a nation-wide case of over-zealous growers who are just excited to help you fulfill your inner farmer. Either way, don't let a warm day here and there before spring comes to stay lure you into jumping the gun (and wasting time and money).

Not all vegetables transplant well. Some vegetables grow best when sown from seed directly into the ground. If you plan on growing any of the vegetables that need to be sown directly into the ground, make sure the soil is warm enough and that it isn't too wet. FYI: Soil that is too wet will pack and harden, making it difficult, if not impossible, for seeds to germinate and break through the ground.

Vegetables that can be successfully started indoors and transplanted into your garden include:

- Tomatoes

- Peppers

- Broccoli

- Herbs

- Cauliflower

- Eggplant

Vegetables that need to be sown from seed directly into the ground include:

- Potatoes

- Carrots

- Beets

- Onions

- Corn

- Lettuce, Kale, Arugula

- Pumpkin

- Melons

- Radishes

- Turnips

- Asparagus

- Peas

- Cucumbers

- Squash

NOTE: It is not unusual to see cucumber and squash bedding plants. I know people who have used them successfully, but I know even more people who have purchased these plants and ended up disappointed with the outcome.

Once you have the plants or seeds in the ground you are officially a gardener. Now all you have to do is keep them alive and healthy so that you can literally reap the benefits of your efforts.

Chapter Four
Raising Vegetables in a Raised Bed

In almost every garden, the land is made better and so is the gardener.
~Robert Rodale

Over the course of the last several years, raised-bed gardening has become a big thing. There are several reasons for choosing this method of gardening—most of which make gardening easier. Raised-bed gardening isn't the ultimate solution in every circumstance, however, so along with all the pros we'll look at the cons, too.

A lot of the same do's and don'ts that apply to in-ground gardens also apply to raised-beds, so I won't waste time and space repeating it. But if you skipped the last chapter because you didn't think it applied to your situation, now is the time to go back and read it, because most of what I said applies to raised-bed gardening, too. Things like making sure your beds are located near a water hydrant and planting according to the signs of the moon are equally important no matter what kind of garden you have. The criteria for choosing bedding plants over seeds, companion planting, and making sure the soil is workable and healthy are also essentials for successful raised-bed gardening.

Raised-bed gardening—the pros

- Raised beds are easier to keep free of weeds. Because you fill your beds with bagged or bulk garden soil and peat moss, you don't inherit the weeds already growing in the soil.

- Raised beds have healthier soil. Let's face it—no matter how good the soil is in your yard, it's going to have at least a few rocks, and it's a near certainty that you'll need to add some sort of fertilizer and compost to improve the tilth (texture suitable for growing). You'll still add these things to your raised beds, but it will be the only thing there, so you have more control over how healthy the soil is.

- Raised beds usually offer better protection from too much rain. If you build your raised beds properly, they will drain better in heavy rains than in-ground gardens will. You will also have more control over making sure your garden is level, which also helps with drainage issues.

- Raised beds can be high enough to make gardening easier on your back and knees.

- Raised beds reduce the risk of dogs, rabbits, possums, and other critters that often cause trouble for gardeners.

- Raised beds usually add a bit more curb appeal to your landscape. This isn't to say an in-ground garden can't. I, for one, thoroughly enjoy seeing a well-kept garden growing proudly from the ground. But since they require more maintenance in the way of weeding, if weeds get out of control, the garden ends up being an eyesore instead of a masterpiece.

- Raised beds are warmer than in-ground gardens. I know this sounds strange, but the soil in a raised bed usually gets warmer quicker in the spring and stays warmer.

- Moles and gophers won't be a problem in raised bed gardens.

- You will probably be able to grow more food in a raised bed because most raised bed gardens don't need rows big enough to walk through. Instead, this space can be used for planting.

- Raised beds make it easier to contain plants that spread and multiply to a desired area. Things like strawberries, asparagus, and various types of mint are examples of plants that fall into this category.

Raised-bed gardening—the cons

- The positive aspect of drainage can cause soil to dry out too quickly during the hot, dry, dog days of summer. When you don't get rain, you'll have to water your raised beds more often.

- Some things (like corn, okra, and potatoes) don't grow well in raised beds unless they are large and deep.

- Raised beds are more expensive. You have to buy the soil to put in the raised beds as well as the materials to build them.

- Raised beds require more hands-on labor. Raised beds cannot be tilled with a tiller, so you have to turn and work the soil by hand, using a spade, hoe, and rake.

- Raised beds don't take up any less space than in-ground gardens. Think about it—raised or not, a 10x10ft space is going to be 10x10 feet.

When you do the math, the pros outnumber the cons. That's enough to convince some people to use the raised-bed method of gardening. Others don't just look at the numbers. They look at the bigger picture. Do they have the money to spend on building raised beds? Do they have the capability to build raised beds? Will raised beds make it easier to manage their garden?

If you decide to use raised beds, you have to decide what you want to use to build them. Wood is by far the most popular choice, especially treated railroad ties or 2x10 lumber. However, there are other options that you might want to consider:

- Sheets of tin on a 2x4 frame

- Large tractor tires

- Metal livestock tanks

- Cinderblocks

- Discarded dresser drawers

When choosing the materials to create the walls of your raised bed garden, you need to **think about how deep the root systems of your plants need to be**. Unlike in-ground gardens, raised beds have only so much capacity for root systems. This means a raised bed with cinderblock walls won't be deep enough for potatoes, but tin walls on a 2x4 frame that is at least 14-16 inches tall will work just fine. The same principle applies to having a deep enough bed to support root systems for tomatoes. Think about it—you need a deeper bed for tomato plants and onions than you do for lettuce and green beans.

Chapter Five
100% Contained

In every gardener there is a child who believes in The Seed Fairy.
~Robert Brault

Container gardening is a bit more complex than in-ground or raised-bed gardening. This has less to do with the plants than it does with you, the gardener. Container gardening requires a higher level of management, but there are also some advantages to container gardening that make the additional management seem insignificant.

If you choose container gardening as a means to grow your own herbs and vegetables, there are two words that need to be first and foremost in your vocabulary: **soil** and **drainage.**

The soil you put in your pots has to be potting soil. **Nothing else will do**. Potting soil is what the name implies. It is meant to be used in pots. Potting soil is less dense. It contains little to no actual dirt/soil, but is a combination of peat moss, vermiculite or perlite, sand, and even finely ground tree bark. This mix of ingredients promotes drainage and even water distribution to ensure plants get just the right amount of moisture. Potting soil has also been put through a sterilization process to kill any weeds and seeds that would interfere with plant growth.

The use of potting soil in your containers isn't the only thing you need to do to ensure proper drainage for your container vegetables. The containers you use **must have adequate drainage holes.** Potting soil does its job of distributing moisture so that the nutrients in the soil are activated, so to speak. But if the container doesn't have adequate drainage holes for the water to escape, it will pool in the bottom of the pot, causing root rot. I don't think I need to tell you that if the roots of a plant are sick (rotting), they cannot feed the plant. And if the plant doesn't get fed, it will die.

Container gardening specifics

At the risk of sounding like a broken record, many of the basic gardening rules that apply to in-ground and raised-bed gardens also apply to raising vegetables in containers. Unless your container gardening consists of only a couple of tomato plants and a few varieties of your favorite herbs, container gardening is more labor intensive than other types of gardening. Containers usually need to be watered and fertilized more frequently than in-ground and raised-bed gardens do. The need for more frequent water, of course, is because the soil tends to dry out quicker in pots than soil in the ground or in raised beds. Or maybe I'd better say it this way: the soil *should* dry out quicker. If it doesn't, you have a drainage problem. With all that extra watering, the nutrients from the soil are being washed away sooner than they can all be absorbed by your seeds and plants.

Container gardeners need to follow these basic gardening rules, just like their in-ground and raised-bed gardening peers:

- Keep the soil weed-free.

- Make sure your containers are accessible to a hose and sprinkler wand.

- Containers need to be large enough to accommodate full-grown plants and their root systems.

- Follow the seeds and bedding plant rules of thumb.

- You need to choose varieties (seeds or plants) specifically developed for container gardening. (This rule doesn't apply to things like lettuce, most herbs, and potatoes.)

- Your containers need to be deep and wide enough to accommodate the vegetables you want to grow.

- Planting by the phase of the moon is always best.

- Companion planting may or may not be an issue, depending on the size of the container.

The whimsy of container gardening

I'm the kind of person you would think of when you see a t-shirt that says something like…

- I play in the dirt

- My garden is my happy place

- Have Garden… will smile

- No Farms… no food

- Got corn? Thank a gardener

Gardening really is my happy place. I love the process and the results. I also love the creativity it brings out in me. In my humble opinion, gardening is an art form.And just like there are multiple mediums for creating works of art, there are countless things you can use to make your container garden an artistic aspect of your landscape. Exercising your creativity gene (and yes, we all have one … somewhere) for the purpose of putting together a container garden can be a lot of fun.

While there is no shame in using simple clay pots, plastic tubs, or large buckets for growing vegetables in containers, it can be a lot of fun to add some whimsy and artistic flare to your yard, patio, or porch by playing around with creative containers. Here are just a few ideas:

- Antique bathtubs

- Replacing the bottoms of old wooden chairs with buckets

- A child's wading pool

- Old graniteware

- Cinderblocks

- Galvanized tubs

- Old boots

Any of the above, along with countless other ideas will make your container garden something people can't help but notice. But you need to keep in mind that ultimately, your goal is to raise at least a little bit of food for your table, so you might want to spend a little more time thinking in terms of practicality and functionality than aesthetics.

You also need to keep in mind that not all containers are suitable for all types of vegetables. You don't want to end up with containers that can't sustain your plants—like Charlie Brown's Christmas tree couldn't sustain one little ornament. Putting equal thought into how much space your plant needs *under* the surface of the soil is as important as thinking about how tall it will grow or how big it will bush out. When you do, you realized that a wading pool is great for growing lettuce and other greens, radishes, green beans, and even miniature pumpkins. You will also understand that the back of an old chair can do the job of a tomato cage when a 5-gallon bucket replaces the seat of the chair and becomes home to a tomato plant. You will understand that a row of old cowboy boots can be filled with potting soil and become a garden row for sweet or hot pepper plants (one in each boot). You will know that an antique bathtub or livestock water tank is deep enough to grow root crops, along with beans, tomatoes, and squash.

Now let's go back to what I said a few paragraphs ago about practicality and functionality. I'll be the first one to say your garden needs to look good, but I'm talking about keeping it weed-free, and keeping the soil somewhat loose to enable better plant growth, water absorption, drainage, and absorption of nutrients into the soil.

Practicality doesn't have to be ugly, though. For example, using large plastic storage tubs (with holes drilled in them for drainage) are perfect for container gardening. They are deep enough to grow anything that can be grown in a container and they come in all colors. Plastic tubs or buckets are a good choice when it comes to watering. Plastic doesn't pull water out of the soil like clay, wood, and cinderblocks do. Plastic also stays cooler than tin or clay. Both of these attributes make for healthier plants and less work on your part.

By now you should have a pretty good idea of vegetables that can and can't be raised in a container with appropriate depth and drainage. But just to make sure you don't set yourself up for disappointment, make sure stick to the following fruits, veggies, and herbs in your container garden:

- All herbs will grow in pots

- Strawberries

- Tomatoes (Tiny Tim, Patio Roma, and other varieties specifically for containers)

- Peppers (any type of pepper)

- Cucumbers (bush varieties developed for containers)

- Miniature melons (Baby Sugar Melon, for example)

- Broccoli, Cauliflower, Cabbage

- Any type of green

- Onions (they generally won't get any bigger than bulb-size)

- Potatoes (they generally won't get very big)

- Carrots (mini varieties)

- Beets

- Radishes

- Peas (varieties for containers)

- Squash (varieties for containers)

- Eggplant

- Celery

Fruits and veggies that won't do well in a container are:

- Corn

- Okra

- Pumpkins (except miniatures)

- Large melons

- Asparagus

- Blueberries

- Raspberries

- Blackberries

- Fruit that grows on trees

- Sweet potatoes/yams

- Turnips

- Parsnips

- Gourds

Planting essentials for container gardening

When planting your garden in containers, you need to follow the same rules for spacing your plants and thinning them once the seeds germinate and start growing. You cannot expect to get the same amount of beans from a couple of 2x3ft storage tubs as you do from two 10ft rows in an in-ground or raised-bed garden. You need to give each plant the room it needs when it is full grown. Overcrowding your plants will result in poor plant growth, reduced productivity, and smaller, spindlier plants and produce.

Remember: Read and follow your seed packets and bedding plant labels for sowing and growing instructions.

Chapter Six
Gardening Vocabulary and Beginner's Manual

No matter where you are you can grow something to eat. Shift your thinking and you'd be surprised at the places your food can be grown! Window sill, fire escape and rooftop gardens have the same potential to provide impressive harvests as backyard gardens, greenhouses and community spaces. ~Greg Peterson

Before we get into the particulars on how to grow and harvest specific types of vegetables and herbs, I want you to become familiar with some general gardening words and terms. These are words you need to know in order to be a successful gardener. As you read through them, you will notice I've already used several of them. In each case I have either provided you with a simple explanation or definition, or it is a word you already know. By repeating them here, I'm not trying to make you feel like a complete gardening dummy. I just want to make sure all the bases are covered and not leave you hanging.

Aeration: Aeration is a word that simply means 'to add air' to something. In this case, that 'something' is the soil for your flower or vegetable garden. Soil that is compacted by constant or heavy foot-traffic, large root systems, or even too much pounding rain, needs to be aerated. This means it needs to be loosened up so the air (oxygen) can flow through it. Why? Because the soil needs oxygen in order to produce the organisms plants need to feed off of.

Companion planting: Planting different types of plants together so that both (or all) can benefit from being next to one another

Compost: Rotted and decaying plant or other organic matter that can be used to fertilize and nourish the soil

Fertilizer: Plant and soil food/nutrients

Germination: The point at which a seed begins to grow

Hardening off: Introducing plants that have been started indoors (or in a greenhouse) to the outdoors. This is also done with houseplants that are brought in each winter and placed outside in the spring.

Heirloom: Plants (usually vegetables) that are reproduced through natural or open pollination. Heirloom plant seeds reproduce the same kind of plant. Example: Yellow Pear tomatoes and Top Crop bush-style green beans are heirloom varieties.

Hybrid: A plant that has been produced by carefully and deliberately cross-pollinating two different varieties of the same plant. Planting hybrid seeds will not yield the same results as the plants from which it came. Example: Early Girl tomatoes are hybrid, as is Peaches and Cream corn.

Irrigation: Slowly and consistently supplying water to plants and soil

Perlite: Tiny bits of obsidian rock used to help retain moisture in soil and promote plant growth

Pesticide: Chemicals or organic substances used to rid plants of harmful insects

Ph level: The amount of acid in the soil

Planting zone: A designated area for growing based on the average growing season (length of growing season, average high and low temperatures, average first and last frost dates)

Pollination: Fertilization of a flower, fruit, or vegetable. Pollination happens as a result of wind, insects, birds, and artificially by people. The male pollen is joined with the female stigma to form a seed. The seed is usually surrounded by either the blooms of a flower or a fruit or vegetable. Example: zinnias, apples, peppers.

Prune: Cutting back excess growth of a plant in order to reshape the plant, control its growth, and concentrate the plant's nutrients where they are needed most

Rootbound: A root ball that is compacted in its container, prohibiting proper growth and nutrient distribution

Seedling: A seed that has developed two sets of leaves

Self-seeding: Plants that drop their seeds onto the soil during the growing season, leaving the seeds to stay dormant in the ground until the following year. The seeds that come up are known as 'volunteers.'

Thinning: Removing excess seedlings so that the plants are not too crowded and to allow a few plants to get proper nutrition so that they will grow full and lush

Tilth: The condition or suitability of soil for growing

Vermiculite: A mineral useful in aiding water retention in soil

Volunteers: Plants that grow from seed left in the ground from the previous growing season

Worm castings: Worm poo—useful for fertilizing the soil

Building your garden

In-ground… raised-bed… container, which will it be? Will it be a combination of two, or maybe even all three? Once you decide what type of garden you want, how big it will be, and where it will be located, *and* once you have the space ready for planting, and know what you want to plant, you can start planting.

Take a look at the pictures below. Do you notice how the vegetables are in rows? How the rows are straight and there is room to walk between each one (in the in-ground garden)? Do you notice how each garden is organized and structured?

Laying out or plotting your garden and sowing the seeds and bedding plants correctly are both essential to its success and vitality. Both of those words—success and vitality—are words I want you to be able to use when describing your gardening experience. To help make that happen, I've put together a mini beginner's manual of planting instructions. Following these basic instructions will not only benefit the plants, it will make managing and harvesting your garden easier for you. And in this case, easier = more enjoyable.

Container gardens

Let's start with the simplest method of gardening when it comes to planting—the container garden. I've already given you a few specifics, but let's take a minute to go over them again and add a few more things to the list of do's and don'ts.

- Planting in rows is not an issue to be concerned with.

- Follow spacing and planting depth rules for planting in containers just like you would in a raised bed or in the ground. You will find the information on seed packets, bedding plant tabs, and in the next chapter of this book. Examples: Don't put more than one pepper plant in a pot that is smaller than 18 inches in diameter. Beans need to be planted 1-2 inches deep approximately 8 inches apart.

- To see if watering is necessary, stick your thumb down into the soil. If it is dry down the entire length of your thumb, you need to water.

- You also need to pay attention to the plants themselves. If they look wilted or their leaves are curling under, you need to give the plant a drink.

- Don't let the soil in your pots become packed down. Use a hand trowel to keep the soil broken up around your plants, taking care not to damage the roots.

- Weeds are generally not an issue, but just in case, get rid of them.

- You can either follow the rules for fertilizing I've included in this chapter, or the instructions on the label of the fertilizer you purchase.

- Composting is not something you can really do while you have plants growing in your pots, but if you have a compost pile or container, you can use the compost in the soil when you prepare the containers for planting at the beginning of the growing season.

- Watching for and getting rid of garden pests is done the same way it is for in-ground and raised-bed gardens. For more information on garden pests, see the **pest control** section of this chapter.

Raised beds

Raised-bed and in-ground gardens are planted and managed similarly, depending on the size and shape of the raised-bed garden. For example, a raised-bed garden built from railroad ties is going to require the same amount of hoeing and weeding as an in-ground garden. On the other hand, if you have a raised-bed garden built out of tractor tires (among other things), you will probably need to use a hand trowel to keep the soil around the plants worked up (loosened), as there won't be enough room to maneuver a hoe. When it comes to things like weeding, pest control, plant care, and harvesting, it's pretty much all the same no matter what kind of garden you have. Keeping that in mind, there are some things you need to know about raised beds:

- Raised beds should be planted in rows. In most cases, the rows of a raised-bed garden will be much shorter than those in an in-ground garden.

- Plant or seed spacing and depth rules should be followed as given in chapter seven of this book or on the labels of your seeds and bedding plants.

- You need to keep the ground around the plants loose to aid in water and nutrient absorption into the soil.

- Pest control and fertilizing in your raised-beds should be done according to the guidelines in this chapter and/or by following the directions on the label of products you buy for these purposes.

- You know you need to water if the soil is dry one to two inches below the surface. You can check by sticking your thumb in the soil. If it is dry down the entire length of your thumb, water your garden.

- You need to pay attention to the plant for tell-tale signs of thirst. If the plant is drooping or its leaves are curling, give it a drink.

- Keep your garden area free of weeds. NOTE: When pulling weeds, don't just throw them on the ground and don't add them to your compost. Get rid of them. Put them in a yard waste bag and take them to wherever you dump your yard waste, OR keep them in a bucket or bag and burn them when you have enough for a small fire in your fire pit or burn barrel.

In-ground garden

Preparing the ground for an in-ground garden takes more time and effort than the other types of gardens, but once that is done, an in-ground garden doesn't have to take any more time or energy to manage and care for than a raised-bed garden. It all comes down to that old saying, "An ounce of prevention is worth a pound of cure." In other words, if you spend a little bit of time every day caring for your garden, you won't have to spend a lot of time in any one day trying to get it back into shape. With that being said…

- Your garden needs to be planted in rows. Planting in rows is the only logical way to keep your garden organized and in good shape.

- To form your garden rows, use a hoe to make mounded rows* across the width of your garden. You can put two rows close together (8-10 inches apart), but make sure you have 12-18 inches on either side of them. This will give you enough space to walk between them to weed, check for pests, fertilize, and harvest. EXAMPLE: If you are planting 4 rows of beans, put 2 rows close together with a wider space on either side. The 2 that are close together will grow so that it will be hard to distinguish between the two rows, but it will still be easy to pick the beans from both rows if you have plenty of room on either side. This method of planting will also give you more planting space in your garden.

*Mounded rows (see below) are a trick of the trade not everyone takes advantage of, but should. Mounded rows provide better drainage, which in turn helps prevent seed from rotting in the ground before it germinates and reduces the risk of root rot in the event of heavy spring rains that leave water standing in the garden. Mounded rows make it easier for you to walk between the rows of your garden and keep the soil around the plants from getting too compacted. Mounded rows or hills are also best for vining crops (cucumbers, pumpkins, melons, etc.).

This gardener is making mounded rows with a tool specifically for that purpose. You can achieve the same results with a hoe or garden tiller.

- Plant or seed spacing and depth rules should be followed as given in chapter seven of this book or on the labels of your seeds and bedding plants.

- Keep the ground around the plants loose to aid in water and nutrient absorption into the soil.

- Pest control and fertilizing should be done according to the guidelines in this chapter and/or by following the directions on the label of products you buy for these purposes.

- You know you need to water if the soil is dry one to two inches below the surface. You can check by sticking your thumb in the soil. If it is dry down the entire length of your thumb, water your garden.

- You also need to pay attention to the plant for tell-tale signs of thirst. If the plant is drooping or its leaves are curling, give it a drink.

- Keep your garden area free of weeds. NOTE: When pulling weeds, don't just throw them on the ground and don't add them to your compost. Get rid of them. Put them in a yard waste bag and take them to wherever you dump your yard waste, OR keep them in a bucket or bag and burn them when you have enough for a small fire in your fire pit or burn barrel.

Pest control

Picture this: a strawberry bed with hundreds of beautiful red berries 'showing off' under a canopy of their green leaves. I squat down to start picking. Most of them are just fine, but every once in a while, I pick one up that looks perfect from the top, only to find the bottom of it has been gnawed on by a slug or some other pesky varmint. How dare they?

Or what about the tomato you watched grow bigger and bigger on the vine, then slowly but surely start to ripen. You were patiently waiting for it to ripen. Then with only a few days left to wait, you discover a bright green caterpillar (tomato worm) has eaten a hole in *your* tomato and is starting on his second helping!

Bugs and worms aren't the only pests that can turn your garden into a disaster area. Rabbits can eat the tops off your green beans quicker than you can imagine. Turtles will eat your melons, low-growing tomatoes, and berries. Deer and raccoons will eat your corn and deer also find beans to be a tasty treat. Birds will peck at your berries, the blooms on your beans, peas, and peppers, and moles will sometimes destroy your root crops.

There are several things you can do to keep pests from destroying your garden. Some are proactive, meaning you take preventative measures to keep bugs and other pests from finding their way into your garden. Some, however, can only be done once you discover you have a problem.

If you take the time to check your plants on a daily basis, curing a problem will be a lot easier, because you'll be able to take action before the problem gets out of hand. Think of it like this: you don't take medicine for a headache every day just in case you happen to get one. But when you *do* get one, you take something for it right away, so it doesn't get worse.

Four legged critters like deer, raccoons, and rabbits can be deterred rather easily (in most cases) by scaring them off. My fellow gardeners and I have found the following to be highly effective in getting rid of these garden thieves:

- A good old-fashioned scarecrow

- Ceramic or metal owl attached to a pole in the same fashion a scarecrow would be

- Cats or dogs made from metal, wood, or concrete, placed strategically in the garden. FYI: Painting their eyes with glow-in-the-dark paint is an added deterrent. It makes them seem more real at night, when most animals do their damage.

- Loud wind chimes, or aluminum pie tins that are allowed to blow in the wind

- Marigolds, mothballs, and human hair scattered around the circumference of your garden or in your containers

Birds can be kept at bay using the same methods (minus the marigolds, mothballs, and hair) listed above.

Insects and worms are the biggest smallest problem you will have as a gardener. They are the epitome of the saying, "Dynamite comes in small packages."

I'm not going to attempt to list all the potential problem-making bugs and worms you might meet in your garden. Instead, I am going to stick to the most common culprits, because that's what this book is about—the basics.

The most common insects and worms you need to be ready to battle with are:

- Slugs

- Aphids

- Japanese beetles

- Stink bugs

- Potato bugs

- Cabbage worms and cabbage white butterflies

- Squash bugs and squash vine bores

- Grasshoppers

- Tomato hornworms

- Cucumber beetles

- Corn worms

- White flies

- Mealy bugs

- Red spider mites (and other mites)

- Codling moth

- Weevils (larvae eat roots and adults eat leaves)

- Caterpillars

- Cutworms

Japanese beetle

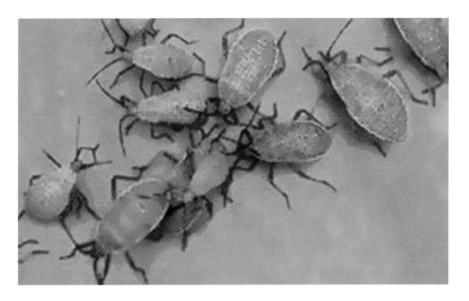

Squash bun on pumpkin

Spider mite damage

Aphids

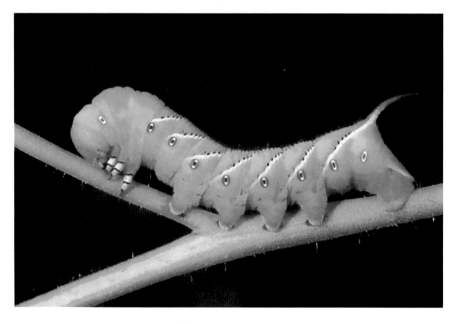

Tomato worm

Whiteflies

Slug

There is no one single method for getting rid of every species of garden pest, but there are a few things you can do to keep most of them away:

- SPRAY your plants. One of the most effective pest control sprays is SEVIN®. It is a broad-spectrum spray that kills the vast majority of problematic insects in your garden. It is a chemically-based product, so you need to wash your produce well before eating if you use SEVIN®, but trust me when I say there is a reason it has been one of a gardener's best friends since 1958.

- Spraying your plants with a solution of Dawn® dish soap and water (1-2 tablespoons per 1 gallon of water) is highly effective in killing all sorts of garden pests—especially aphids and mites.

- Neem oil, which is a natural product taken from the neem tree is effective in killing several garden pests. You can purchase it, as well as other types of natural and chemically-based products and should follow the instructions on the label.

- GOOD BUGS can be introduced into your garden to eat the bad bugs. I know, to many of you, the words 'good' and 'bug' seem like an oxymoron, but they're not. There are several bugs you actually want in your garden.

- KEEP YOUR GARDEN WEEDED. Keeping your garden weed-free isn't just about making it look good. Weeds attract bugs you don't want in your garden.

  - Ladybugs

  - Earthworms (not bugs, but still VERY good for your garden)

  - Bees

- Praying mantis

- Soldier bug

- Dragon fly

- Green lacewing

- Ground beetles (black)

- HERBS: Lavender, lemon balm, mints, garlic, thyme, catnip, and rosemary are among the herbs that discourage pest invasions.

- FENCING might be necessary to keep dogs, deer, possums, and rabbits out. If you have chickens, the fence will keep the chickens from pecking at your plants and produce, too.

Fertilizer is food for the soil and your plants. When fertilizing your garden, you need to remember that over-eating is just as detrimental to plants as it is to your own body. There are two ways to fertilize your garden: **naturally or processed.**

- Natural fertilizers include worm castings (poo), compost (see below), and cow, rabbit, or chicken manure.

- Processed chemical fertilizers are fertilizers made from nitrogen, phosphorus, and potassium. When you buy fertilizer, you will see three numbers on the package. The numbers are usually 10-10-10, 7-7-7, or 10-5-10. These numbers indicate the ration of NPK—always in that order. Processed fertilizers come in liquid, powder, or granular form. They can be sprayed, sprinkled on the ground around the plants, or mixed with water used to water your plants.

You don't have to limit yourself to one specific type of fertilizer. A lot of gardeners keep a compost pile throughout the year, and add it to their garden at the beginning of the growing season. They follow up with processed fertilizer throughout the growing season as needed.

When choosing a **processed fertilizer,** it is best to stick with name-brand products that have a proven track record. When looking for proven success, it will be impossible to ignore the Miracle-Grow® name. No, this is not a paid endorsement, or an unpaid one for that matter. But you can't ignore the facts and the facts about fertilizer are that these people know what they're doing.

Going back to what I said about being careful not to over-feed your plants, take a look at this over-fertilized tomato plant:

Do you notice how the leaves are discolored but aren't curling or dry and crumbling—except on the tips where the combination of too much fertilizer and heat have baked them? This plant is getting the right amount of moisture and doesn't appear to have been bothered by pests. The problem here appears to be too much of a good thing—over-fertilizing.

You can also over-fertilize by adding manure to your garden that is too 'hot,' meaning it has not dried and decomposed enough. The fertilizing effects (nitrogen, phosphorus, and potassium content) of manure are much stronger when the manure is still wet. You will know the manure is not too hot when it crumbles in your hand or when using a garden tool to break it apart.

Composting

Now let's move on to the subject of **compost.** Composting is collecting organic material for the purpose of letting it decompose (rot). In its decomposed state, it adds important nutrients to the soil. Your compost pile can be as simple as a designated area in your yard to pile compost matter, or it can be more sophisticated, i.e. a well-ventilated wooden box, plastic tub, or barrel.

There are numerous things you can put in your compost pile to enrich your garden's soil. Compostable materials include:

- Fruit and vegetable peelings

- Egg shells

- Coffee grounds

- Stale beer

- Corn meal and oatmeal

- Pet and human hair

- Old spices

- Dead leaves

- Grass clippings

- Dead plants (as long as they aren't diseased)

- Stale bread

- Tea grounds and tea bags

- Peanut shells

- Dryer lint

- Toilet paper cardboard tubes (paper towel tubes, too)

- Cow, chicken, horse, sheep, or rabbit manure

Other than piling the compostable materials together and occasionally turning or stirring them with a shovel or pitchfork, there's not much work involved in composting; it's a natural process.

Tools of the trade

Walking into the gardening section of the home supply store or garden center can be confusing if you don't know the difference between a spade and a shovel or a pitchfork and a rake. Are garden clippers different from lopping shears? Are all sprinklers the same? And do I really need one of each?

No, you don't need one of each, but there are differences in some garden implements that make it necessary to have the basics on hand. The following is a list of what are considered to be the essentials for successful gardening:

- Garden rake

- Leaf rake

- Rounded shovel

- Sharp-shooter shovel (sometimes called a spade)

- Hoe

- Hand trowels (rake and shovel style)

- Heavy-duty hose

- Sprinkler- Make sure it is heavy enough to not hop and jump around when you turn the water on, and that it has various settings.

- Watering can

- Watering wand that will attach directly to the hose and has a number of different settings

- Sprayer (hand-held and/or backpack style)

- Garden stakes

- Tomato cages

- Garden twine

- Clippers

- Lopping shears

- Garden gloves

- Buckets for carrying water, mixing fertilizer, holding weeds, etc.

- Garden weasel and/or tiller appropriate for the size of your garden

Taking the time to prepare and plant your garden properly gives you and your plants the best possible start. Taking some time every day to tend to your garden is your insurance policy for success and an enjoyable, tasty, and fulfilling new hobby.

Chapter Seven
Let's Get Growing

A gardener's best tool is the knowledge from previous seasons. And it can be recorded in a $2 notebook. ~Andy Tomolonis

In this chapter we are going to look at the specifics of planting, growing, and harvesting different vegetables. Some of the information will seem repetitive. That's because it is. The information you need for one vegetable is often the same for many others, but because not all of us grow the same things, it's necessary to give every veggie equal attention.

I'm not including every vegetable a person might have in their garden, because there just aren't many people out there interested in growing spaghetti squash, lemon cucumbers, or parsnips. However, I will try to mention as many as possible where appropriate.

IMPORTANT: In several instances, I state that bedding plants should be used instead of sowing seed directly into the ground. If, however, you have the time, space, and proper conditions for starting your own bedding plants from seed, you can do so with the following vegetables: peppers, eggplant, tomatoes, broccoli, cauliflower, and cabbage.

There are others that I haven't included in this beginner's manual, so if you want to plant something not listed here, contact your local county extension agent or reputable garden center. You can also visit the following website: https://www.almanac.com/gardening/growing-guides.

This website gives you a thorough overview of the most common problems specific to each vegetable, how to avoid and deal with the problems, soil and water conditions favored by each type of vegetable, and a list of varieties that are easy to grow.

NOTE: When removing the bedding plant from its container, gently squeeze the outside of the container from the bottom to loosen the soil and roots from the sides the container's sides. This should also cause the plant and soil to slide out of the container so you can carefully plant it—soil and all.

Potatoes: Potatoes are planted by digging a trench about 8 inches deep and placing potato pieces with eyes (buds) in the trench with the buds on top, 12 inches apart. Cover the potatoes with the soil.

If you want to harvest new potatoes, which are small, walnut-sized potatoes, you can do that 2-3 weeks after the plants stop blooming. For mature potatoes, after the plants die, cut the tops, wait 3-5 days, and then dig your potatoes. Be careful not to puncture the skin of the potato. If you do, you need to use them within a few days. Potatoes can be stored in a cool dry place—never in the refrigerator and not near apples.

- NOTE: Some people cover their potatoes with 2-3 inches, wait for the plant to poke through the soil, and then cover the rest of the way. This is not a must; whichever method you want to use is fine.

- NOTE: Seed potatoes (potatoes with lots of buds) can be cut into pieces. Just make sure there are at least 2 buds on each piece you plant and that you plant it cut side down.

- NOTE: If the seed potato is smaller than an egg, plant the whole thing.

- NOTE: When cutting seed potatoes, cut them a day or two before planting to give the cuts a chance to heal over.

- NOTE: Keep the dirt hilled over the base of the plant to protect the potatoes growing in the dirt.

Sweet potatoes/yams: Sweet potatoes and yams are planted in a trench like potatoes are, 8-10 inches deep and 12 inches apart. Time from planting to harvest is 3-4 months. Aside from that, here is what you need to know:

- Instead of planting pieces of sweet potato, you will plant 'slips.' Slips are leafy stems that grow from the eyes of a sweet potato.

- To propagate sweet potato slips, you need to purchase unblemished sweet potatoes and place them in a jar, filling the jar halfway with water. Place the jar(s) in a sunny location and replace the water as necessary. This is best done in November and December to have slips ready for spring planting.

- By planting season, the slips should be 10-12 inches long. Carefully break the slip off the potato and plant as you would a potato.

- Potatoes can be harvested once the leaves of the plants turn yellow/brown and the plants wither. You harvest sweet potatoes and yams the same way you do potatoes.

Onions: Onions are grown using onion sets, which are tiny onion bulbs that usually have tops (the green stem). Using the handle of your hoe or your thumb, make a hole 2 inches deep, place one bulb in each hole and cover, leaving the top exposed. Pack the dirt lightly to hold it in place. Space the onions 6 inches apart. Don't worry that the tops of the onion sets are brown and limp. As they begin to grow, new tops will sprout out of the ground.

You can harvest your onions in late summer or early fall before the ground freezes. NOTE: You can also cut some of the tops throughout the summer to add to salads and pico de gallo.

Carrots: Carrots are sown from seed directly into the ground, as you cannot transplant a carrot. Carrot seeds should not be sown very deep—no deeper than 1 inch. Simply make a little trench on top of your mounded row, scatter the seed down the row and cover over with dirt using your hand. Be sure to pack lightly to hold the seed in place.

Once the seeds sprout, you will probably need to thin the plants. This is done by carefully snipping up a few of the plants so that there are 2-3 inches between them. Carrots can be harvested 2-3 months after planting, depending on the variety you plant.

NOTE: Make sure you don't dump or pour water directly on the seed, but rather let the water 'drizzle' from a sprinkler so as not to wash the seed away.

Beets: Beets are planted, managed, and harvested in the same way carrots are. The only exception is the time to harvest. Beets are harvested about 60 days after planting.

Squash: Squash should be planted from seed, as plants do not transplant well. You will see squash bedding plants in garden centers, but I strongly advise against going that route. The roots are just too tender and susceptible to damage.

Squash seeds should be planted the same way you plant beans, 2 inches deep. But instead of planting in rows, it is usually best to plant squash in hills. To make a hill, make a mound of dirt 6-8 inches tall with a circumference of 12-18 inches. Make 3 holes and place 3 or 4 seeds in each hole.

Because there are so many varieties of squash, you need to refer to the individual seed packets to know how large the squash needs to be before harvesting, but most squash are ready to harvest 50-60 days after planting.

Eggplant: You can purchase bedding plants when planting eggplant. To transplant your bedding plants, make a hole in your mounded row big enough to accommodate the soil the bedding plant is in. Make sure it is deep enough to cover 1-2 inches of the stem that is currently exposed, leaving a space of 10-12 inches between plants.

Eggplant is ready to harvest 4-5 months after planting, or when the skin is bright, shiny, and unwrinkled. NOTE: The eggplant skin will not bounce back when you press gently with your thumb.

You will need to cut the eggplant stem, as it is too thick to break off. Trying to break it will damage your plants.

You also need to be aware of the fact that eggplant is heavy, making it necessary for you to stake your plants to keep them upright.

Peppers: Pepper plants should be planted as bedding plants. They should be planted deep enough to cover 1-2 inches of the stem and be spaced 14-16 inches apart. If you are growing bell peppers, you might want to stake your plants to keep them upright.

You can harvest peppers when they reach the desired size. In the case of bell peppers, the longer you leave them on the plant (as long as they don't start to shrivel), the sweeter they will be.

Corn: Corn seed must be planted directly into the ground. Use the handle of your hoe to make holes along the top of your mounded rows. Drop 2-3 seeds in each hole, spacing them 12 inches apart, and lightly pack the dirt on top to hold the seeds in place.

Corn will be ready for harvest when the tassels are brown and dry, and the cobs are 'swollen.' You can gently pull the tassels down to reveal the top inch or so to see if the kernels are plump and juicy. If so, it's ready. You can expect this to happen around 90 days after planting

Okra: Okra should be planted from seed. Seeds should be planted 10-12 inches apart, 2 or 3 in each hole. Pack the dirt lightly to hold the seed in place. The blooms of the okra plant are pretty and showy. Once they start appearing watch for the okra to appear. This usually starts 2-3 months after planting.

When looking for okra to harvest, look carefully, as it tends to 'hide' by hugging the stalk. Sometimes this results in not seeing it until it is too large to eat. Okra is best eaten when it is 3-4 inches long.

NOTE: Some people snip the bottom leaves off the okra stalks once it starts bearing. They say it produces a heavier crop.

NOTE: Make sure you leave lots of space between your rows of okra and/or between the okra and whatever you plant next to it. The reason for this is that the okra leaves and stalks are extremely hairy/prickly. When it touches your skin, it will feel itchy and cause a slight burning or irritation. For that reason, I usually wear long sleeves when cutting the okra from the plants.

Tomatoes: Tomatoes can be grown from bedding plants. Plants should be sown about 2 feet apart and planted to a depth that covers the bottom set of leaves on the stem. It is also a good idea to remove an additional set of leaves from the bottom of the plant, in order to help the plant be more productive. To remove the leaves, gently pinch them off, being careful not to break into the stem's flesh.

Depending on the variety of tomato you grow, they are usually ready for harvest 60 days or so after planting. You will know they are ready when they are bright red or yellow (depending on the variety) and shiny. The skin should also bounce back a bit when pressed gently. This tells you the flesh is juicy and ready to be eaten. If the tomato is blistered or wrinkled, it has been left on the plant too long.

Peas: Peas must be started from seed and sown in the same fashion as beans—2-3 peas in a hole 2 inches deep. Space the plants 10-12 inches apart.

Peas are ready 6 to 8 weeks after planting. Once you have harvested them, pull the plants and plant a second crop that will be ready in early fall before the first frost in most planting zones.

You will know the peas are ready when you see them bulging out the sides of their pods. You can also pick them earlier, if you want to eat the baby peas and their tender pods.

Beans: There are numerous varieties of beans—green, wax, purple hull, pinto, etc. Beans are easy to grow and will supply you with an abundance of fresh, delicious goodness. You should always plant beans from seed (beans) sown directly into the ground. They should be sown 1-2 inches deep, 8-10 inches apart. The easiest way to plant the beans is to use the handle end of your hoe to make holes in your rows, drop the seed in, cover it with dirt, and pat it lightly to seal the hole. Beans are usually ready to pick around 60 days after planting.

Be mindful of what type of bean you are planting—bush or pole. Bush beans grow low to the ground (10-12 inches tall). The beans will be under the canopy of leaves. Pole beans are climbers. They will need trellises for their runners to climb. Beans will be on the runners and in and among the leaves.

Melons: Melons should be planted from seed in mounded hills rather than rows. To make the hill, mound the dirt 6-8 inches high with a circumference of 18 inches or so. Plant 3-4 seeds in a hole 2 inches deep—3 holes per hill.

Melons take approximately 3 months to mature. You will know the melon is ready to pick when…

- The stem is hard and dry. If it's green, it's not ripe, but if it's hard and dry, it might be over-ripe, so check your melons daily.

- The bottom has a yellow or yellow-brown patch of skin. White means it isn't ripe.

- It sounds hollow when you thump on it.

- There is a bit of 'give' when you press on the stem end or bottom of the skin.

- Cantaloupe should give off a slight scent of the melon. Too much, though, and it is over-ripe.

Melons do well when the ground around them has a heavy layer of mulch or straw. The added layer of padding wicks excess moisture away from the melons so they don't rot, prevents weeds from growing up around the melons, and gives the vines a little extra something to cling to.

NOTE: Melons are especially needy of pollination, so be kind to the bees. To attract the bees to the area, you might want to consider planting flowers nearby to help attract the bees to your garden.

Pumpkins: Pumpkins should be started from seed. They should be sown the same way melons are. Make a hill and mound the dirt 6-8 inches high with a circumference of 18 inches or so. Plant 3-4 seeds in a hole 2 inches deep—3 holes per hill.

Pumpkins can be harvested when they are bright orange. This usually takes about 90 days. If you want pumpkins for fall decorating and Halloween, you need to plant them in June or July.

NOTE: Pumpkins need lots of space and nutrients. They are, as some gardeners put it, the neediest of all vegetables.

Cucumbers: Cucumbers need to be started from seed and sown in hills with the same depth and spacing as squash. Cucumbers, like melons, have a particularly strong need for bees in order to pollinate properly. If your cucumbers aren't producing, it's most likely a pollination problem, so you will need to take steps to attract bees to the area.

Cucumbers spread their vines across the ground, so it's necessary to provide them with plenty of room. If you would rather train them to climb trellises, you can do so, but it will take early intervention to get them growing in an upward motion.

NOTE: When training your cucumbers to climb the trellises, make sure you don't break the stem, causing serious damage to your plants.

Cucumbers should be harvested when they are 6-8 inches long. Leaving them to get longer and fatter only makes them bitter. The exception to this rule is burpless cucumbers. They need to be allowed to grow to 8-10 inches long. Cucumbers are usually ready to harvest 50-60 days after planting.

NOTE: There are now varieties of cucumbers that are specifically for container gardens and those that are categorized as bush cucumbers instead of the traditional vining varieties.

Broccoli: Broccoli bedding plants are among the vegetables you can plant the earliest. I myself am not one to plant early crops. I prefer to wait until the soil and air temperatures allow me to plant everything at once, with the exception of pumpkins.

Plant your broccoli in rows, making sure the bottom of the plant is securely 'sitting' on the soil. Plants should be placed 2 feet apart, as they need plenty of room to develop into large, round heads with several layers of foliage surrounding the edible florets. It usually takes 80-90 days for broccoli to be ready to harvest.

NOTE: Broccoli plants are easily infested, so diligence is the key to keeping them healthy.

NOTE: Don't be alarmed if your broccoli plants send off shoots that start to grow smaller heads of broccoli. Let them grow—the more the merrier.

Cauliflower: Cauliflower is planted from bedding plants and is tended and harvested in the exact same manner as broccoli.

Cabbage: Cabbage is planted from bedding plants, also using the same depth and spacing as broccoli and cauliflower (deep enough to ensure the plants are sitting on the soil and about 2 feet apart).

Cabbage is also highly prone to infestation and must be guarded closely.

Cabbage can be harvested about 70 days after planting, when the heads are firm and about the size of a child's head, or slightly smaller. Like broccoli, cabbage is prone to forming multiple heads, giving you more to eat and enjoy.

Lettuce and other greens: Lettuce and other greens must be sown from seeds directly into the ground. To plant, after forming your mounded row, 'scratch' the surface of the top of the row, scatter the seed, pat the surface of the dirt lightly to hold the seed in place, and watch it grow.

You need to be careful about watering your lettuce in its beginning stages. Don't dump or pour water on your lettuce/greens. The water needs to hit it like a gentle shower, so as not to wash the seeds away.

Most greens are harvested 30 days or so after planting. The quick 'return' on your efforts makes it easy to have 2 crops of lettuce each year.

NOTE: Don't let the lettuce leaves get too big, or they get bitter.

Asparagus: Asparagus can be grown in a raised bed or directly in the ground. Asparagus is a perennial plant, meaning it comes back year after year without having to be planted again. It also multiplies itself. It usually takes 2 to 3 years for asparagus to become prolific enough to harvest, but it is well worth the wait.

Asparagus is started from 'crowns,' which are year-old plants/ roots. Because it is a perennial plant, it needs to be planted in a place it won't be bothered or in the way of tilling the ground for the rest of your garden each year.

To plant: In early spring, dig a trench about 8 inches deep. Place the crowns tip-side up in the trench about 8 inches apart. Fill the trench with soil, keep weeded, and leave it alone.

FYI: Asparagus has male and female plants. The females produce red berries in the fall filled with hundreds of seeds. The seeds will germinate, but it will take 2 to 3 years for plants from seeds to sprout spears big enough to eat. NOTE: the berries are highly toxic, so don't eat them.

REMEMBER...

No matter what you decide to plant in your garden, it is important to remember the following:

- Once you've planted your seeds or bedding plants, you need to be mindful of how you work the soil. The roots of young plants are very tender. Damaging them is a death sentence to your plant.

- Mature plants are only as healthy as their roots. Keep the soil loose, properly watered and fed, and make sure you treat the plants with care. Don't be too rough in handling them.

- The information I've given you is accurate and correct but should be paired with instructions specific to the variety of plants you choose to grow.

HAPPY GARDENING!

Closing Comments

I hope this book heightens your interest in gardening and encourages you to try your hand at raising a few vegetables for you and your family to enjoy. There's nothing quite like seeing bits of green poke through the soil, knowing you are the one who made it happen. And then those little bits of green grow into a fully mature plant that produces something you can actually sink your teeth into. The satisfaction and pride you feel makes every drop of sweat and the moments spent meticulously pulling weeds worth it.

With that being said, GROW... EAT... GROW SOME MORE!

Resources for Gardeners

Old Farmer's Almanac:
https://www.almanac.com/content/2019-old-farmers-almanac
The OFA is also available in print form.

Your county extension office and Farm Service Agency

Your state's department of agriculture

"You Grow, Girl": http://yougrowgirl.com/

"Dave's Garden":
https://davesgarden.com/guides/pf/https://davesgarden.com/g uides/pf/

If you've enjoyed reading this book, subscribe* to my mailing list for exclusive content and sneak peaks of my future books.

Visit the link below:

http://eepurl.com/glvBjj

OR

Use the QR Code:

(*Must be 13 years or older to subscribe)

Made in the USA
Coppell, TX
14 November 2020